MOM AND DAD
DON'T LIVE TOGETHER ANY MORE
Text Kathy Stinson
Illustrations Nancy Lou Reynolds

Annick Press Ltd., Toronto, Canada
M2M 1H9

Sixth printing, March, 1989

Annick Press gratefully acknowledges the contributions of
The Canada Council and The Ontario Arts Council

Canadian Cataloguing in Publication Data

Stinson, Kathy
    Mom and Dad don't live together any more

ISBN 0-920236-92-8 (bound) — 0-920236-87-1 (pbk.)

I. Reynolds, Nancy Lou. II. Title.

PS8587.T56M65 1984   jC813'.54   C84-098915-6
PZ7.S74Mo 1984

Trade Distributed in Canada and the USA by:
Firefly Books Ltd.
250 Sparks Ave.
Willowdale, Ontario
M2H 2S4
Canada

Printed and bound in Canada by
D.W. Friesen & Sons Ltd.

TO MY CHILDREN MATTHEW AND KELLY

My mommy and daddy
don't live together any more.

I live with my mommy and my brother in an apartment in the city.

We go to Daddy's house in the country on the weekends.

If I had a wishbone I would wish for us to all live together again. Mommy and Daddy say that will never happen. But I still wish it sometimes.

Dad, I wish you lived in the apartment across the hall so I could see you every day.

I like it at Mommy's apartment.
I like riding the elevators.
I like dropping garbage down the chute.

I like it at Daddy's house too.
I like feeding the horses at the back fence.
I like playing with my old friends.

I wonder if Daddy wants to get married with Paula.

Mom, when I grow up, will I get married and then get apart?

Last summer we went camping with Daddy.

Mommy took us up the CN Tower.

I wonder where we'll be on Christmas.

I hope Santa knows.

Mommy says I make her happy.

Daddy says I make him happy.

I wish I could make them happy together.

I wonder why Mommy and Daddy can't make each other happy.
They say they tried and they can't any more.
That's why they're separated.

I like to be with Mommy.
She puts barrettes in my hair.
She takes me to ballet class.

I like to be with Daddy.
He gives me shoulders.
He takes me to Nana's for dinner.

I love my mommy and my daddy.
My mommy and my daddy love me too.

Just not together.